Sticking Power

Written by Samantha Montgomerie

Collins

Each day, there are lots of risks for living things.

They must look for ways to stay away from risks.

Some living things avoid risks by
sticking to things.

Staying stuck

The foot of the limpet helps it stay stuck.

limpet

foot

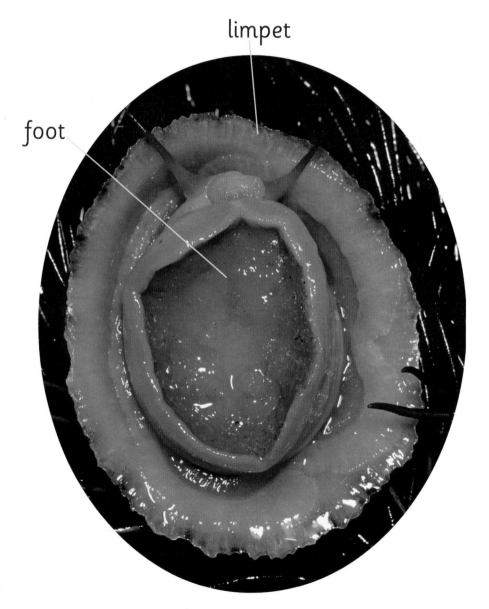

The sea cannot sweep it away from the rock.

Remora fish have sucker pads.
They can stick on to big rays
and sharks.

This remora gets a free lift
as the ray swims away.

Remora are "sharksuckers"

On the go

A trail helps snails stick
as they slither up
and away.

Snails slither to food and shelter high up.

Tree frogs have pads on each foot.
They stick as the tree sways.

There is no risk they will drop off, as the pads keep them stuck on the tree.

Getting food

Lizards grab food with thick spit.

When the lizard sees its food ... flick!
The insect stays stuck to the gloop.

Squid have long arms with suckers to grab food.

Fish stick to the suckers. They cannot get away.

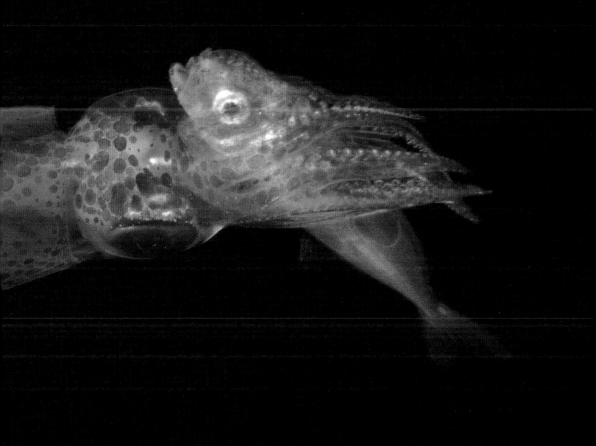

Avoiding risk

This eel digs into the sand with its tail.

Gloop from its tail keeps the eel stuck in the sand.

The hagfish has lots of gloop. This stops attackers killing it.

Sticking helps living things to hunt, avoid risk, flee or stay still.

With gloop, spit, fins or feet, living things have lots of tricks to stick.

Tricks to stick

Staying stuck

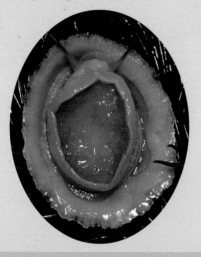

On the go

Review: After reading

Use your assessment from hearing the children read to choose any GPCs, words or tricky words that need additional practice.

Read 1: Decoding

- Challenge the children to find words where the /ai/ sound is spelled "ay".
  - o Set a timer for one minute. How many different "ay" words can they find? (e.g. *day, ways, stay, away, staying, rays, sways*)

Read 2: Prosody

- Model reading each page with expression to the children. After you have read each page, ask the children to have a go at reading with expression.
- On page 13 show the children how you pause for the ellipsis to add suspense and use a surprised tone for the exclamation mark.

Read 3: Comprehension

- Turn to pages 22 and 23 and use the pictures to talk about how something sticky helps the animals.
- For every question ask the children how they know the answer. Ask:
  - o On pages 4 and 5, why does the limpet need to be stuck? (e.g. *so that the sea doesn't wash it away*)
  - o On pages 6 and 7, why is the remora called a "sharksucker"? (e.g. *because it sticks itself to sharks*)
  - o On pages 8 and 9, why do snails leave a trail? (e.g. *so that they stick as they move, so that they can move high for shelter*)
  - o Which animal do you think has the cleverest trick? Why?

Getting food

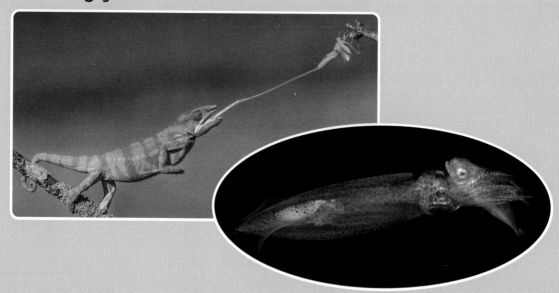

Avoiding risk

23